Guide to the Federal Credit Bureau Program

A Companion to the Treasury Financial Manual Credit Supplement

Department of the Treasury
Financial Management Service

Guide to the
Federal Credit Bureau
Program

**A Companion to the
Treasury Financial Manual
Credit Supplement**

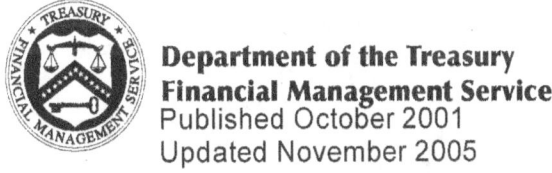

Department of the Treasury
Financial Management Service
Published October 2001
Updated November 2005

TABLE OF CONTENTS

PREFACE

CHAPTER 1

INTRODUCTION

CHAPTER 2

REPORTING CONSUMER ACCOUNT INFORMATION

CHAPTER 3

REPORTING COMMERCIAL ACCOUNT INFORMATION

TABLE OF CONTENTS

APPENDICES

PREFACE

The use of nationally recognized credit reporting agencies (also known as credit bureaus) is an inexpensive tool that can assist Federal agencies to improve their credit management and debt collection programs. While only one of several tools available, increased credit bureau reporting and increased Federal agency use of credit reporting agencies is designated as a "high priority" by the Office of Management and Budget (OMB), the Treasury Department's Financial Management Service (FMS), and the Federal Credit Policy Working Group.

Reporting delinquent Federal debts to credit reporting agencies makes good financial management sense. This action enables Federal agencies to *prevent* individuals and businesses from obtaining credit or entering into business relationships with one Federal agency while owing an outstanding unresolved delinquent debt to another. Conversely, the reporting of *current* debt information on individuals and businesses that are paying their bills to the Government in a timely manner helps these individuals and businesses benefit from their *positive* credit history.

The credit report continues to emerge as a formidable tool in Federal agencies' credit management and debt collection arsenals and as part of the Federal Government's program to reduce outstanding delinquencies. Federal program agencies can access accurate data from credit reporting agencies to conduct credit screening and the collection and verification of tax identification numbers. Further, credit reports are used to conduct credit scoring, skip tracing, and asset determination. Now that any participating lender in a Government-insured or guaranteed loan program is required to report the extension of credit, a truer credit picture will be reflected on a credit report. Also, the credit report, when used in conjunction with other Federal credit management and debt collection tools (the Department of Housing and Urban Development's (HUD) Credit Alert Interactive Voice Response System [CAIVRS], tax refund and administrative offset and referrals to the Department of Justice), helps Federal agencies and the participating lenders to avoid approving additional loans which would overextend an applicant beyond his/her ability to make repayment.

The goals of the Government pertaining to credit and debt management activities can be accomplished if Federal agencies observe the guidelines contained in this document. Reporting the Government's entire debt portfolio, to include *current* and *delinquent* debts, ensures that all relevant Federal debtor data are integrated into credit reporting agency databases and are available for consideration when credit decisions are being made.

Finally, taxpayers' confidence will increase as the public becomes aware of the Government's commitment to making sound credit decisions and reducing its delinquencies. Reporting debts to credit reporting agencies is an important step in this process. Correct use of credit reporting agencies, whether when required or as encouraged, is the direct responsibility of the respective Federal agency; the intent of these guidelines is to assist in meeting those responsibilities. Additional information regarding the submission of Federal debtor data to credit reporting agencies can be found in <OMB Circular No. A-129 - Policies for Federal Credit Programs and Nontax Receivables>, the <Federal Claims Collection Standards> published jointly by the Departments of Treasury and Justice, and the Financial Management Service publication <Managing Federal Receivables>.

Richard Gregg
Commissioner
Financial Management Service

Purpose of Guidelines

These guidelines apply to <u>ALL</u> Federal Executive, Legislative and Judicial agencies, including Government corporations. The purpose of this document is to provide guidance to Federal agencies for reporting information on Federal debts (consumer and commercial) to designated credit reporting agencies. The guidelines are consistent with the Debt Collection Act of 1982 (DCA), as amended by the Debt Collection Improvement Act of 1996 (DCIA), the revised Federal Claims Collection Standards (31 CFR Parts 900-904) published November 22, 2000, the revised Office of Management and Budget (OMB) Circular No. A-129 published November 29, 2000, and the Financial Management Service (FMS) publication "Managing Federal Receivables" (revised May 2005). Relevant portions of the DCA and the DCIA are codified at 31 U.S.C. § 3711(e) (see **Appendix 1**) and 3720(B).

This document supersedes the previous "Guide to Federal Credit Bureau Reporting" which was published in 1991. This guide will be periodically updated to include new information as it develops.

Since 1991, numerous changes have occurred, most notably:

(a) The DCIA, enacted in 1996, requires agencies to report to credit reporting agencies, information on **all** delinquent consumer debts owed to the Federal Government;

(b) The DCIA authorizes agencies to report accounts in good standing to credit reporting agencies. Reporting accounts in good standing ensures that <u>all</u> relevant Federal debtor data is integrated into the credit reporting agency databases and is available for consideration when credit decisions are made and prevents overextension of credit;

(c) The DCIA requires that lenders financing and/or extending credit on behalf of the Federal Government be required to provide information relating to the extension of credit to consumer and commercial credit reporting agencies. Submission of debtor information to designated credit reporting agencies should be a routine and ongoing part of Federal agencies and certified lenders account servicing **and** debt collection procedures for both consumer and commercial accounts;

(d) The revised Federal Claims Collection Standards, published in November 2000 clarify and simplify Federal debt collection procedures (and reflect changes under the Debt Collection Improvement Act of 1996 and the General Accounting Office Act of 1996); and

(e) The "Metro 2" format for reporting consumer debt, developed by the credit reporting industry, is designed to capture better data for debtor records within the credit reporting agency databases. The Metro 2 format increases the accuracy of debtor files which subsequently produces a better credit report and provides additional features for the report user. The format is the industry standard for providers of information. See Chapter 2 for additional information on the Metro 2 format.

The Financial Management Service (FMS) is available to meet with Federal agencies to assist with the reporting effort, including facilitation of the Memoranda of Understanding (MOUs) between Federal agencies and the designated credit reporting agencies receiving Federal debtor data. "Model" consumer and commercial MOUs are located at **Appendix 2. The MOUs in Appendix 2 can can be reproduced and used to enter into agreements with the credit reporting agencies.** Contacts for credit reporting agencies and FMS are listed in **Appendix 3**.

In addition to this document, the following materials provide guidance on reporting to credit reporting agencies:

•• OMB Circular No. A-129 **"Policies for Federal Credit Programs and Non Tax Receivables"** (Revised);

•• **"Federal Claims Collection Standards"** (Revised) (See 31 C.F.R.§ 901.4); and,

•• FMS Publication **"Managing Federal Receivables"**(Revised May 2005).

Agencies should review Office of Management and Budget (OMB) Circular No. A-129 for policies on the use of credit reports for the purpose of screening and determining creditworthiness of applicants for Federal financial assistance or persons seeking to do business with the Government.

Background

The Debt Collection Act of 1982 gave agencies the authority to report delinquent nontax, non-tariff consumer debts to credit reporting agencies provided that Federal agencies follow detailed procedures.

The DCIA was enacted through the cooperation of major Federal Government credit granting agencies, the OMB, the Chief Financial Officers Council and the Department of the Treasury. The DCIA significantly enhanced the Debt Collection Act of 1982. The DCIA **requires** Federal agencies to report to credit reporting agencies, information on all delinquent Federal consumer debts. The DCIA also **authorizes** the submission of information on consumer debtors considered as **"current."** Federal agencies have been required, as a matter of policy, to report **all** (current and delinquent) commercial debts since September 1983.

This requirement was subsequently incorporated into OMB Circular A-129 and the Federal Claims Collection Standards. As detailed later in this document, agencies are encouraged to report their entire debt portfolios (current and delinquent debts).

Definitions

A "**claim**" or "**debt**" (used interchangeably) means any amount of money, funds or property that has been determined by an appropriate official of the Federal Government to be owed to the United States by a person, organization or entity other than another Federal agency. Section 3701(b) of Title 31 of the United States Code defines a **"debt" or "claim"** to include:

- funds due to the United States on account of loans made, insured or guaranteed by the Government, (including any deficiency or difference between the price obtained by the Government in the sale of a property and the amount due to the Government on a mortgage on the property);

- expenditures of non-appropriated funds;

- overpayments;

- any amount the U.S. is authorized by statute to collect for the benefit of any person;

- the unpaid share of any non-Federal partner in a program involving a Federal payment and matching or cost sharing payments by the non-Federal partner;

••   fines or penalties assessed by an agency; and

••   any other amounts of money or property due to the Government other than delinquent taxes and tariffs.

"**Accounts receivable**" are generated by **all** Federal agencies. **Examples of accounts receivable are**: fines, fees, penalties, forfeitures, royalties, audit disallowances, claims, rents, damages, overpayments, and other amounts owed to the Government.

"**Credit reporting agency**" (also known as "**credit bureau**")- Major consumer and commercial credit reporting agencies that have signed agreements Memoranda of Understanding (MOUs) with Government agencies to receive and integrate credit information (data) from voluntary subscribers (Federal agencies and private sector entities) into their respective database. In turn, this information is sold, oftentimes by smaller credit reporting agencies, to purchasers of credit data (in the form of credit reports and other products). The credit report, etc., is used to determine creditworthiness, conduct credit scoring, assist with collection efforts, or for other permissible purposes as defined by the Fair Credit Reporting Act. (See **Appendix 3** for designated credit reporting agencies.)

"**Non-exclusive basis**" - Federal agency debtor account information is reported to **each** of the designated credit reporting agencies receiving Federal debtor data. (Agencies should attempt to resolve issues which prevent reporting in this manner.)

Distinction between Commercial and Consumer Debt

In accordance with the definitions contained in "Managing Federal Receivables," the term "commercial" signifies a business activity and the term "consumer" signifies a personal activity. **The purpose of the activity, not the type of entity involved, determines whether a debt is classified as commercial or consumer**.

For example, a loan to a farmer to obtain additional land or equipment for farming would be considered a commercial loan; whereas a loan to the same farmer to purchase a personal residence would be a consumer loan.

When to Report Debts to Credit Reporting Agencies (Reporting Cycle)

There are four points in the credit management and debt collection cycle when Federal agencies should make use of credit reporting agencies. As part of its financial management responsibility, an agency should report information on its Federal debtors to credit reporting agencies in the following circumstances:

When to Report Debtor Information

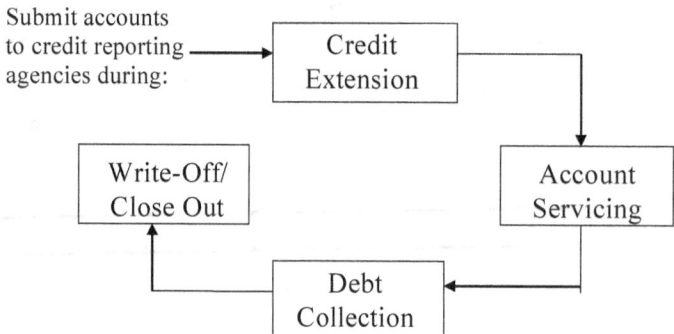

•• **Credit Extension** - Under the DCIA heads of agencies must, as a condition for insuring or guaranteeing any loan, financing, or other extension of credit under any law to a person, require that the lender provide information relating to the extension of credit to consumer reporting agencies or commercial reporting agencies, as appropriate. Additionally, pursuant to 31 U.S.C. § 3720B, Federal agencies may not grant a loan or loan guarantee to a person or entity which owes delinquent nontax debt to the Federal government. See 31 C.F.R. § 285.13. Agencies are required by OMB Circular No. A-129 to screen potential applicants for Federal financial assistance for creditworthiness. The applicants' credit history (credit report) also becomes a part of the official loan origination files. In instances where a delinquent Federal tax or nontax debt has been reported and is reflected in the applicant's credit history, agencies should immediately suspend loan processing (unless statutorily prohibited). In instances where the loan, etc. has been approved, the indebtedness should be reported to a credit reporting agency after funds have been disbursed.

•• **Account Servicing** - Once a loan is awarded and disbursed, or a financial obligation to repay an administrative debt has been established, the Federal agency (or in the case of a guaranteed loan, the lender) becomes responsible for servicing or controlling the account. Federal agencies may provide to consumer reporting agencies or commercial reporting agencies information from a system of records that a person is responsible for a claim which is current. If account servicing has been contracted out or a lender is servicing the account, agencies must require the servicer or lender to make the initial referral of debtor account information to credit reporting agencies and to provide accurate and consistent account status updates.

•• **Debt Collection** - Reporting debts to credit reporting agencies is an essential part of an agency's debt collection efforts. In accordance with Federal law, agencies must report information on all Federal delinquent consumer debtors to credit reporting agencies. Regulations and policies governing commercial debtors are covered in OMB Circular No. A-129 (revised November 2000) and the Federal Claims Collection Standards (revised November 2000). With some exceptions, Federal agencies must not extend credit assistance to debtors owing unresolved delinquent debts to the Government (see 31 U.S.C. § 3720B and 31 C.F.R. § 285.13). When debts have been transferred to FMS or a designated debt collection center for collection pursuant to the DCIA, FMS or the debt collection center, as appropriate, will perform debt collection activities (which include referral of accounts to credit reporting agencies if requested by the transferring agency).

Prior to reporting delinquent consumer debts to credit reporting agencies, agencies must provide consumer debtors certain rights of due process which are detailed in Chapter 2, "Reporting Consumer Account Information."

•• **Write-Off and Close-Out** - An effective receivables management program must include the systematic write-off and close-out of uncollectible debts pursuant to OMB Circular A-129. Essentially, once the debt is written-off, the agency must either classify the debt as currently not collectible (CNC) or close-out the debt. If an agency determines that continued collection efforts after write-off are likely to yield higher returns in the future, then the debt is not closed out but classified as CNC and reporting to credit reporting agencies should continue. Once the agency determines it is no longer cost effective or legally possible to pursue collection, the debt should be closed-out and all collection activity ceased. The account's status is forwarded to the credit reporting agencies receiving Federal data. Agencies should consult OMB Circular A-129 for details.

"Individual Service Agreements" and Memoranda of Understanding (MOUs)

In past years, many agencies signed "Individual Service Agreements" with credit reporting agencies to accept, store and integrate Federal data into credit reporting agency databases. While FMS does not require termination of these agreements, the Memoranda of Understanding (MOUs) promote standardization of the reporting process government wide and are consistent with current law. Agencies are encouraged to enter into the MOUs at the expiration of their current service agreements. The MOU should be signed by the Federal agency Chief Financial Officer or the designee and the appropriate credit reporting agency official. Federal agencies should also have their counsel review current agreements to determine whether they are compliant with current law and policy.

The MOUs obligate Federal agencies to provide credit information on their accounts to the particular credit reporting agencies signing the MOU. In turn, the credit reporting agencies agree to accept, load, store, and incorporate this information into their data files and credit information. This ensures that when a Federal agency or private sector lender purchases a credit report on an applicant or debtor, the Government's information is reflected in the report purchased.

Obtaining Credit Reports

The smaller credit reporting agencies authorized by the General Services Administration (GSA) on the Federal Supply Schedule (FSS) to provide credit reports for Federal agencies **must** purchase their information from the designated credit reporting agencies listed at **Appendix 3**. Federal agencies **should** use the FSS for the purchase of credit reports and related information, unless circumstances dictate otherwise. Purchasing credit reports through the FSS is no different from purchasing other items through the GSA's FSS.

Agencies are required by OMB Circular No. A-129 to purchase credit reports for screening loan applicants. Where appropriate, Federal agencies should obtain information (credit reports) on loan applicants from both commercial and consumer credit reporting agencies prior to extending credit or other Federal assistance. Credit reports should also be purchased at other times throughout the credit cycle:

•• to verify a debtor's claim of financial inability to pay a debt in a lump sum, as is required prior to entering into an installment agreement;

•• to reassess a debtor's financial position when considering rescheduling a debt or otherwise entering into a workout agreement;

•• to evaluate administrative offset and other debt collection possibilities; and

•• to meet the requirement that an agency provide credit data on a debtor when referring a debt for litigation.

The agency's cost to purchase a credit report or other credit information should be passed along to the borrower/debtor: (a) through the application fee when used to determine creditworthiness and eligibility during credit extension; and, (b) as an administrative cost when used after the debt becomes delinquent.

Credit Bureau Reporting Made Easy

Action Required	Consumer Reporting	Commercial Reporting
1. Sign Memoranda of Understanding (MOU) with credit reporting agencies (see "Model" Memoranda of Understanding at **Appendix 2**) facilitated by the Financial Management Service, Debt Management Services. See **Appendix 3** for Treasury/FMS contact information.	YES	YES
2. Contact the consumer and/or commercial credit reporting agencies receiving Federal debtor data to establish reporting relationship (contacts, addresses, etc.). Agencies are reminded that data should be sent on a non-exclusive basis (data should be sent to **each** of the credit reporting agencies). See **Appendix 3** for credit reporting agency contacts.	YES	YES
3. Agree with each credit reporting agency on the method in which data will be sent. (tapes, disks, electronically, etc.)	YES	YES
4. Prepare data for submission to credit reporting agency. **NOTE**: Reporting Cycles **Consumer - Report Monthly**-(more frequent updates may be made as required) **Commercial - Report Quarterly**-(more frequent updates may be made as required)	YES	YES
5. Complete "Transmittal of Account Information" sheet to accompany tape, etc. (Attachment A to MOU)	YES	YES
6. Submit data to credit reporting agencies. The credit reporting agencies will return all tapes to the respective agency after the data has been loaded into the respective databases. Agencies are encouraged to work to establish procedures to ensure that the information has been loaded and is being properly reported by the credit reporting agencies.	YES	YES
7. Prepare quarterly report to Financial Management Service (Attachment B to MOU).	YES	YES

Special Rules/Laws	Consumer Account Data	Commercial Account Data
The Privacy Act of 1974, as amended - Promotes greater governmental respect for the privacy of citizens.	YES	MAY APPLY*
Debt Collection Act of 1982 (DCA) - Increases the efficiency of government wide efforts to collect debts owed to the United States and to provide additional procedures for the collection of those debts.	YES	YES
DCA due process requirements include: Requirement for 60-day notice to debtor before submission of delinquent debtor data to credit reporting agencies. See Chapter 2 - Reporting Consumer Accounts	YES	N/A
Debt Collection Improvement Act of 1996 (DCIA) - Requires the reporting of all nontax delinquent consumer debts to credit reporting agencies.	YES	N/A
The DCIA authorizes the reporting of current consumer and commercial debts.	YES	YES
OMB Circular No A-129, dated November 29, 2000 - Provides regulatory guidance consistent with the DCA and the DCIA regarding the referral of accounts to credit reporting agencies. Instructs agencies to report all current and delinquent commercial debts.	YES	YES
The Department of the Treasury, Financial Management Service's "Managing Federal Receivables" - provides program guidance to Federal agencies on reporting of information to credit reporting agencies.	YES	YES
Justice/Treasury "Federal Claims Collection Standards"- dated November 22, 2000 - Regulations governing Federal debt collection procedures (including the use of credit reporting agencies).	YES	YES

*Consult with Agency Counsel

Reporting Consumer Accounts

The purpose of this chapter is to provide general instructions for reporting account information on **consumer debts** to credit reporting agencies.

Special Rules for Reporting Consumer Account Information

The reporting of information on individual consumers is governed by certain laws, regulations and policy guidance, including:

•• **The Privacy Act of 1974** as amended - Promotes greater governmental respect for the privacy of citizens.

•• Debt Collection Act of 1982 (DCA) as amended by the **Debt Collection Improvement Act of 1996 (DCIA)** - increases the efficiency of government wide efforts to collect debts owed to the United States and to provide additional procedures for the collection of those debts.

•• **DCIA** - The DCIA **requires** the reporting of **all** non tax **delinquent consumer** debts to credit reporting agencies. **The DCIA also authorizes** the **reporting of current consumer and commercial debts**.

•• **OMB Circular No. A-129** - Provides regulatory guidance consistent with the DCA and the DCIA regarding the referral of accounts to credit reporting agencies.

•• Justice/Treasury **Federal Claims Collection Standards** - regulations governing Federal debt collection procedures (including the use of credit reporting agencies).

•• The Department of the Treasury, Financial Management Service's **Managing Federal Receivables** - includes guidance to Federal agencies on reporting information to credit reporting agencies.

Legal Requirements

Federal agencies are legally required to follow certain procedures when reporting delinquent **consumer** debts to credit reporting agencies. Prior to reporting a delinquent consumer debt to a credit reporting agency, a Federal agency must:

•• comply with the provisions of the Privacy Act of 1974. See 31 U.S.C. § 3711(e)(1)(A). Agencies should consult their counsel in order to comply with Privacy Act requirements.

• establish procedures to:

  – disclose promptly to consumer reporting agencies substantial changes in the condition or amount of a debt;

  – verify or correct promptly information about a debt on request of a consumer reporting agency for verification of information (see section entitled "Handling Disputed Information in Consumer Debtor Files"on page 2-5); and

  – get satisfactory assurances that consumer reporting agencies are complying with Federal laws related to providing consumer credit information. See 31 U.S.C. § 3711(e)(1)(E).

- •• take reasonable action to locate a person about which the information will be reported for whom the agency does not have a current address. See 31 U.S.C. § 3711(e)(3).

- • review the debt to be reported and decide that the debt is valid and overdue. See 31 U.S.C. § 3711(e)(1)(B).

- • determine that the person about which the information will be reported has not:

    - – entered into a written repayment plan with the Federal agency; or

    - – filed for a review of the debt. See 31 U.S.C. § 3711(e)(1)(D).

- • send a notice to the person about which the information will be reported at least 60 days prior to reporting a debt to a credit reporting agency (see "60-day Notice of Intent to Report to Credit Bureau," below) and notify the person that he or she is entitled to a complete explanation of the debt, to dispute information in the records about the debt, and to an administrative repeal or review of the debt. See 31 U.S.C. § 3711(e)(1)(C).

- • provide for a review of the debt upon request, including an opportunity for reconsideration of the initial decision. See 31 U.S.C. § 3711(e)(2).

60-Day Notice of Intent to Report to Credit Bureau

Pursuant to 31 U.S.C. § 3711(e), when reporting information on delinquent consumer accounts, the debtor must be notified 60 days in advance of such reporting to the credit reporting agency. Agencies should provide this notice in the initial billing notice or demand letter, but no later than the second demand letter sent by the agency.

The notice must include:

- •• the agency's intent to report the debt to a credit reporting agency;

- •• the specific information to be transmitted (i.e., name, address, and taxpayer identification number, information about the debt);

- •• the actions which may be taken by the debtor to prevent the reporting (i.e., repayment in full or a repayment agreement).

- •• the rights the debtor has under 31 U.S.C. § 3711 to a complete explanation of the debt, to dispute the debt, to review records about the debt, and to seek an administrative repeal or review of the agency's determination that the debt is due.

NOTE: Agencies must also comply with any requirements contained in any contract, agreement, law or regulation applicable to the debt.

Once all due process procedures have been observed, (i.e., the demand letter(s) have been sent, the debtor has been given 60-days to respond to the notification of intent to report to a credit reporting agency, and either the debtor has not responded or any disputes have been resolved, an agency **must** report the debt to the appropriate credit reporting agencies. (See **Appendix 3** - Credit Reporting Agency Contacts).

Handling Disputed Information in Consumer Debtor Files

Consistent with 31 U.S.C. § 3711(e), debtors shall have the right to dispute inaccurate information contained in their files and the right to review records pertaining to their debts.

Reporting debts owed to the United States to consumer reporting agencies is governed by the DCA and the DCIA as codified at 31 U.S.C. § 3711(e). Obligations of consumer reporting agencies and state and local government agencies to investigate disputes under the Fair Credit Reporting Act (FCRA) arise independently of 3711(e). Federal agencies should be aware that credit reporting agencies may be required by the FCRA to delete information if their investigation is not completed within 30 days.

It is critical for agencies to perform their investigations in a manner that will allow completion within 30 days and prevent deletion of the information. The standard procedures for resolving disputes by credit reporting agencies are depicted on the flow chart shown on page 2-7 titled "Summary of Procedures Disputing Accuracy of a Credit Report". The 30-day clock starts the day the credit reporting agency receives a dispute from a debtor in writing, by phone, or in person. Credit reporting agencies then have five (5) days to provide the notice of dispute and all relevant information to the Federal agency. Given that most responses back to the credit reporting agencies from Federal agencies will be by mail, a three to five day mail time allowance is required. Once the mail times are deducted this provides Federal agencies approximately 20-22 days after receipt of the dispute to resolve and return it to the credit reporting agency on the last day before deletion.

While 31 U.S.C. § 3711(e) does not hold Federal agencies to a specific timeframe, it does require Federal agencies to verify or correct **promptly** information about the claim on request of a consumer reporting agency for verification of information disclosed.

Credit reporting agencies are **not required** to remove accurate data from their files unless it is outdated or cannot be verified. (See chart on the next page which details the consumer dispute process.)

Therefore, Federal agencies should have procedures in place to promptly address such disputes. In order to avoid having information deleted at the expiration of the 30 days, agencies are strongly encouraged to review and make a decision on disputes and report back to the credit reporting agency within **fourteen (14)** days if possible and no longer than **twenty one (21)** days maximum.

SUMMARY OF PROCEDURES DISPUTING ACCURACY OF A CREDIT REPORT*

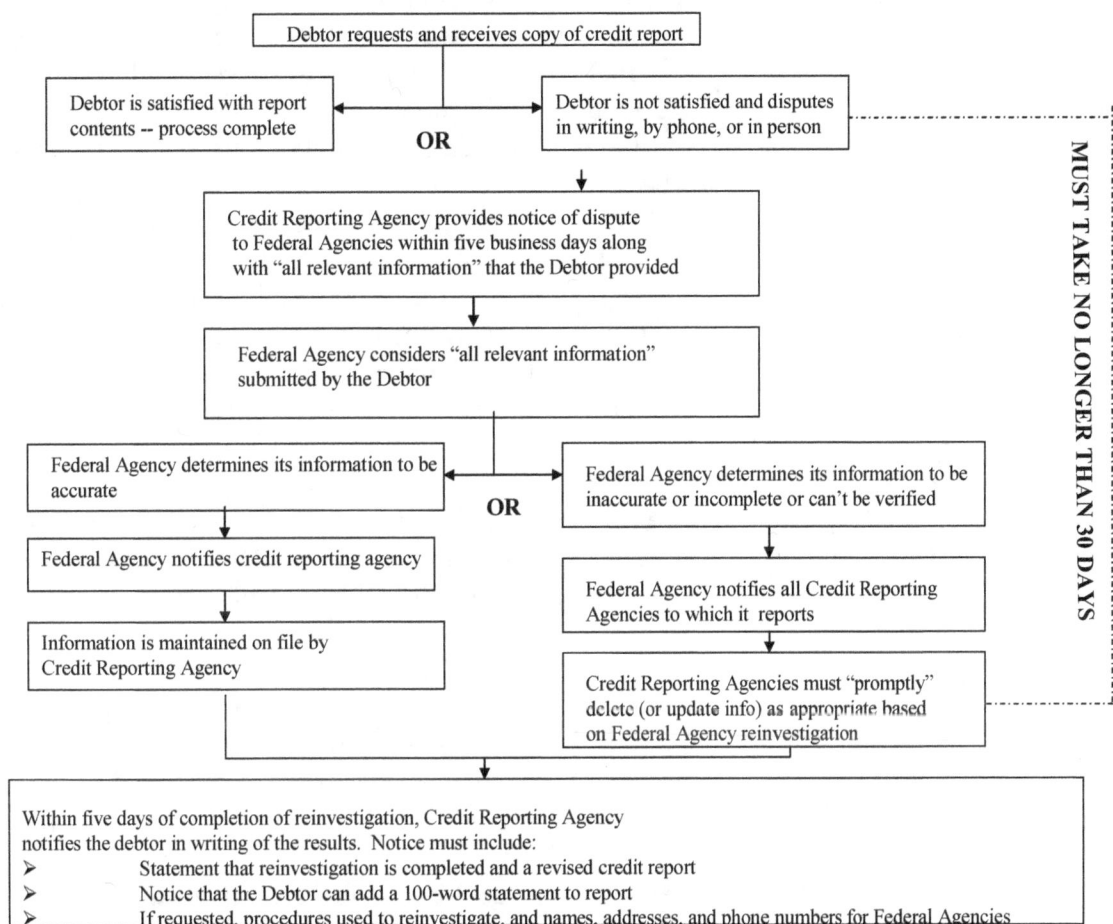

*BASED ON "THE CREDIT REPORTING DISPUTE RESOLUTION PROCESS" WITH PERMISSION OF THE CONSUMER DATA INDUSTRY ASSOCIATION (CDIA)

Procedures to be Used When Consumer Debt Goes from "Current" to "Delinquent" Status

As described earlier in this chapter, Federal agencies must comply with certain due process procedures before reporting a delinquent consumer debt to a credit reporting agency. A minimum of 60 days is required to comply with due process procedures, which include providing the debtor with notice and an opportunity to dispute the information to be reported. See "Legal Requirements" and "60-Day Notice of Intent to Report to Credit Bureau."

This section describes the procedures to be followed when the status of a consumer debt changes from "current" to "delinquent." Federal agency procedures applicable to the due process period (60 days or while appeals and reviews are pending) are as follows:

•• send the 60-day notice described in the above section entitled "**60-Day Notice of Intent to Report to Credit Bureau;**"

•• if the agency has been reporting the debt as "current/not delinquent,"remove the debtor's account from data (tapes, etc.) sent to the credit reporting agencies. In other words, do not report the account;

•• if the debtor asks for a review of the files or disputes the debt, do not report the debt until any reviews or appeals are completed;

•• if the debtor submits a **payment(s) or enters into a repayment agreement <u>within the 60-day period</u>** the account should be updated accordingly;

•• <u>**after passage of the 60-days (or after all reviews or appeals are completed**</u>), report the delinquent account(s) to the credit reporting agencies.

Presumably, this would be the third month of delinquency, since consumer accounts are reported on a monthly basis.

During subsequent reporting periods, the agency should update the debtor's account status. **NOTE:** Generally, Federal agencies are not required to send debtors multiple notices of intent to report to a consumer reporting agency. Agencies should consult their counsel to determine when multiple notices are required.

Reporting Debts Being Collected by FMS' Debt Management Services (DMS)

With some exceptions, the DCIA requires that Federal agencies transfer to Treasury, or a Treasury-designated debt collection center, all debts which are greater than 180 days delinquent (see *31 U.S.C. § 3711(g)*). When a debt is transferred to the Financial Management Service's Debt Management Services (DMS) -- the area within Treasury responsible for collecting delinquent debt--the agency to which the debt is owed (known as the "creditor agency") must certify that it has completed all due process required by the DCIA and Treasury regulations for reporting debts to credit reporting agencies. (See *31 U.S.C. § 3711(e)* and *31 C.F.R. § 285.12* for due process and certification requirements.)

Federal agencies have the option of transferring delinquent debts prior to the expiration of 180 days, provided they have completed all due process requirements, and they certify the debts as required by *31 C.F.R. § 285.12*.

Federal agencies have two options for credit bureau reporting once they have referred cases to DMS for debt collection, a process known as "cross-servicing:" (1) they may continue to report the cases to credit reporting agencies, and DMS will not do so; or (2) they may cease reporting, and DMS will report to credit reporting agencies on the Federal agencies' behalf. Federal agencies are asked to select the option they prefer when completing the "DMS Cross-servicing Agency Profile" form (see **Appendix 4**).

Further information on FMS cross-servicing can be found in the FMS publication "Cross-Servicing Implementation Guide" at: http://www.fms.treas.gov/debt/crosserv.html.

As a part of its regular debt collection procedures, DMS will report debts it is collecting to the appropriate designated credit reporting agencies. If a credit reporting agency notifies DMS that a debtor has disputed the validity or accuracy of a debt, DMS will notify the creditor agency of the dispute. If the creditor agency does not recertify the debt within the specified time, DMS will return the entire debt file to the agency and cease all further collection efforts, including referral to credit reporting agencies. See **Appendix 3** for DMS contact information.

General Instructions

The following applies for all consumer accounts:

•• Prior to reporting delinquent consumer debts, the head of the agency must comply with legal requirements described earlier in the "Legal Requirements Section:"

•• An agency **must report** account information on **delinquent** nontax, non-tariff, **consumer** debts at least **monthly**. Agencies may update account information more frequently to maintain the integrity and accuracy of the information reported. Agencies should report complete information on each debt, not just the updated items.

There is no minimum dollar threshold on the amounts for debts which agencies can report.

••   In accordance with the DCIA, agencies are now authorized to report **current (i.e., not delinquent) consumer accounts to credit reporting agencies**. Consumer information is **reported** on a **monthly basis**. Agencies should report current account data so that debtor files contain **all** indebtedness to the U.S. Government. This information assists debtors who are current when being considered for credit and assists the government when determining the debtor's creditworthiness and ability to repay other obligations (avoids overextension).

••   Agencies should report debtor account information to credit reporting agencies on a non-exclusive basis (i.e., submit account information to each consumer credit reporting agency receiving Federal data) unless circumstances dictate otherwise.

In order to avoid potential reporting errors, agencies should not re-use or re-issue account numbers after an account has been closed.

••   Agencies should report each debt separately and not group together debts owed by a single borrower, regardless of the amount of activity with that borrower.

••   Agencies should report capitalized interest or other capitalized expenses as part of the debt giving rise to the interest or expense. For example, if $1,000 in interest is capitalized on a $50,000 debt, the amount to be reported as a single account would be $51,000.

•• In the case of participation loans (loans consisting of both direct and guaranteed portions or more than one lender), an agency would report only the direct participation amount. The guaranteed amount would become reportable by the agency after the agency acquires the guaranteed portion in satisfaction of a default claim.

•• An agency should furnish the account information electronically, on-line, on magnetic tape, manually, or in any other form agreed to by both parties.

Use of the Metro 2 Format for Referring Information to Credit Reporting Agencies

In 1997, the credit reporting industry initiated the use of the "Metro 2" format which became the industry standard for reporting debtor information. The "Metro 2" format was developed by Consumer Data Industry Association (CDIA) to replace the Metro format which was developed in the late 1970's. The Metro 2 format facilitates complete and greater accuracy of reporting of data and provides the following features:

•• format is designed to be easier to use and understand;

•• allows reporting on debtors that "cannot be located;"

•• allows reporting of deferred payments and "associate" borrowers/debtors information;

•• Identification numbers can be changed to accommodate transfer or sale of debt (asset sales); and,

•• the format accommodates a 4-digit "year" field to accommodate reporting in the year 2000 and beyond.

Reporting Consumer Account Information

The credit reporting agencies receiving Federal debtor data will assist agencies to implement Metro 2 format reporting. (See Appendix 3 for credit reporting agency contacts.)

Electronic copies of the <u>Metro 2</u> reporting format are available from Consumer Data Industry Association (DCIA) via the **<u>Internet</u>** in the following steps:

a)   **INTERNET address: <u>http://www.cdiaonline.org</u>;**

b)   from the home page, click on the "Data Provider/Metro2/ACDV/AUD" icon;

c)   click underneath Metro 2 for Credit Reporting on "Instructions to Access the Metro 2 Format;" The Metro 2 format is posted on the Consumer Data Industry Association (CDIA) website in Adobe Acrobat Reader format, also known as "pdf." Adobe Acrobat Reader will be necessary to open and read the document.

d)   call telephone numbers listed to obtain UserID and passcode.

e)   click on "download" where indicated;

f)   **<u>complete and submit</u>** user/subscriber information;

g)   a prompt that the submittal was successful should be displayed; **select the option to download the format in either "windows" or "MAC."**

h)   type in "**<u>METRO 2</u>**" (uppercase) at the **<u>user</u>**

i.d. prompt; and finally,

i)   type in "**accuracy**" at the password prompt.

The speed at which the file will download depends on the type of modem used with your computer. The file will be downloaded as a "zipped" file which must then be "unzipped" to be opened.

Federal Agency Identifiers

A list of agency identifiers (**Appendix 5**) has been developed for use with the Metro 2 format.

Important Debtor Identification Elements

When preparing information for submission to the credit reporting agencies, the following information is essential to maintaining the accuracy of debtor records:

••   Account Number: This should be the unique alphanumeric or numeric code which identifies each individual loan, loan guarantee, or debt.

Codes which are based primarily on Social Security Numbers are acceptable only if the agency can distinguish between different loans which may have been made, or other types of credit which may have been extended to an individual or entity and if such use of Social Security Numbers is otherwise authorized by law. Agencies have the option of adding an additional character to the code to make such distinctions.

- •• Taxpayer Identification Number (TIN): This is the number used by the Internal Revenue Service to identify individuals and businesses (e.g., Social Security Numbers and Employer Identification Numbers). Agencies are required by 31 U.S.C. § 7701(c) to obtain the TIN of all persons or entities with whom it does business. All agencies and lenders extending credit **shall** require the applicant or borrower to supply a TIN as a prerequisite of obtaining credit or assistance. **NOTE**: Delinquent debts should be reported even if agencies are unable to locate a TIN.

  When transmitting files to the credit reporting agencies, the TIN can be omitted **only** if the Federal agency has exhausted all remedies in efforts to obtain it, and **if** the credit bureau reporting agency agrees to accept the account without it.

- •• Name: This should identify the individual(s) or entity legally liable to repay the debt. Agencies should require the debtor to notify them of any changes made to legal liability for the debt and should maintain, in their files, the names (and addresses) of the debtor of record and all other legally liable parties.

- •• Address: This should be the address of principal residence of the legally liable individual(s) which corresponds to the debtor(s) of record, including city, state and zip code. A street address rather than a route number or post office box should be reported.

- •• Type of Debt: Report the category that best describes this account.

- •• Date of First Disbursement/Date Debt Established: For a loan or line of credit, this is the date when credit was extended by the initial disbursement of funds or the closing on a loan, whichever is earlier.

For other types of debts, the date to be reported is the date on which the event which created the debt occurred or the date the charge was assessed. For example, if the debt arose as the result of an installment sale, then the date of such sale goes in this field. Similarly, the date a fine or fee is assessed would be the date the debt was established. The date the debtor was notified of the debt should not be used unless that is the date the debt was established (e.g. certain administrative debt).

•• Amount: Report the full amount of the original debt and any capitalized interest, principal only.

•• Terms: This is the length of time for which credit has been extended, from the date of the first disbursement of funds until the date of the last originally scheduled repayment by the debtor. Report this time period in years for real estate loans.

•• Association: Report the individual's or entity's relationship to the account, e.g., individual, joint, co-maker, etc. If reporting a relationship other than individual, information must be provided on each legally liable party involved with a debt. If the financing information is the same for all parties, a separate section on the same file must be completed. If the financing information is not the same, then a separate file must be completed for each liable party.

SUMMARY

Federal agencies seeking to establish a reporting relationship with credit reporting agencies should do the following:

1. Execute an MOU with each consumer credit reporting agency accepting Federal data on consumer debts (See Sample MOU at **Appendix 2**).

2. Contact each of the consumer credit reporting agencies receiving Federal debtor data to establish a reporting relationship (contacts, addresses, etc.). Federal agencies are reminded that data is to be sent on a non-exclusive basis (all data is to be sent to **each** of the consumer credit reporting agencies). See **Appendix 3** for credit reporting agency contacts.

3. Agree to method and media in which data will be sent (magnetic tape, disks, electronic, etc.).

4. Prepare data for submission to credit reporting agencies. See Chapter 2 for information on the "Metro 2" format for reporting consumer debt.

5. Complete "Transmittal of Account Information" sheet to accompany tape, etc.

6. Submit data to credit reporting agencies. The credit reporting agencies will return all tapes to the respective agency after the data has been loaded into their database. Agencies are encouraged to work with the credit reporting agencies to develop a method to determine whether debtor data has been loaded into their database and is being properly reported.

7. As required by the DCIA, codified at 31 U.S.C. § 3711(e), Federal agency data furnishers must notify consumer debtors of the agency's intent to report a delinquent debt; supply accurate account information; correct inaccurate information; and research and respond to consumer disputes in a timely manner.

Reporting Commercial Accounts

The purpose of this chapter is to provide general instructions for reporting information on **commercial debts** to designated credit reporting agencies and detailed information on the categories of information to be reported. See OMB Circular No. A-129 for additional information.

General Instructions

The following applies to all commercial accounts:

Pursuant to OMB Circular No. A-129, and the Federal Claims Collection Standards (FCCS), Federal agencies shall report account information on **all delinquent** nontax, non- tariff, commercial debts. Agencies shall also report **current** nontax commercial debts. This information assists debtors who are current when being considered for credit and assists the government when determining the debtor's creditworthiness and ability to repay other obligations (avoids overextension). There is no minimum dollar threshold on the amounts for debts which agencies can report.

•• Account information should be reported on a non-exclusive basis; i.e., debtor information should be submitted to each designated commercial credit reporting agency receiving Federal data, unless circumstances dictate otherwise. (See **Appendix 3** for credit reporting agency contacts.)

•• **Federal agencies will report commercial account information on a quarterly basis.** More frequent updates may be provided as necessary to maintain the integrity and accuracy of the information being reported. Agencies should report complete information on each debt, not just the updated items.

••   An agency should report each debt separately and not group debts owed by a single borrower, regardless of the amount of activity with that borrower.

••   An agency should report capitalized interest or other capitalized expenses as part of the debt giving rise to the interest or expense. (For example, if $1,000 in interest is capitalized on a $50,000 debt, the amount to be reported as a single account would be $51,000.)

••   In case of participation loans (loans consisting of both guaranteed and direct portions or involving more than one lender) an agency would report only the direct participation amount. The guaranteed amount would become reportable if the agency acquires the guaranteed portion in satisfaction of a default claim.

An agency should furnish the account information electronically, on magnetic tape, disks, manually, or in any other media agreed to by both parties. Magnetic tape information should be prepared in the format provided at the end of this chapter. An agency should report all of the information listed in this section (beginning on Page 3-4) for each account. **Agencies currently unable to do so must, at a minimum, provide the information below that is indicated with an asterisk (*)**. This information is essential for the adequate identification of an account. Provisions should be made, however, for providing all items of information as soon as possible.

Requests by the credit reporting agencies for additional categories of information not included in this document should not be honored unless authorized by law, and agreed to by the agency, and the Debt Management Services of the Financial Management Service (FMS) has been informed of the request. See **Appendix 3** for the Debt Management Services contact information.

Reporting Debts Being Collected by FMS' Debt Management Service (DMS)

With some exceptions, the DCIA requires that Federal agencies transfer to Treasury, or a Treasury-designated debt collection center, all debts which are greater than 180 days delinquent (see *31 U.S.C. § 3711(g)*).

Federal agencies have the option of transferring delinquent debts prior to the expiration of 180 days, provided they have completed all due process requirements, and they certify the debts as required by *31 C.F.R. § 285.12*.

Agencies have two options for credit bureau reporting once they have referred cases to the Financial Management Service's Debt Management Services (DMS) for debt collection, a process known as "cross-servicing:" (1) they may continue to report the cases to credit reporting agencies, and DMS will not do so; or (2) they may cease reporting, and DMS will report to credit reporting agencies on the Federal agencies' behalf. Federal agencies are asked to select the option they prefer when completing the "DMS Cross-Servicing Agency Profile" form (see **Appendix 4**). Further information on DMS cross-servicing can be found in the DMS publication "Cross-Servicing Implementation Guide" at: http://www.fms.treas.gov/debt/crosserv.html.

As a part of its regular debt collection procedures, DMS will report debts it is collecting to the appropriate designated credit reporting agencies. If a credit reporting agency notifies DMS that a debtor has disputed the validity or accuracy of a debt, DMS will notify the creditor agency of the dispute. If the creditor agency does not recertify the debt within the specified time, DMS will return the entire debt file to the agency and cease all further collection efforts, including referral to credit reporting agencies. See **Appendix 3** for DMS contact information.

Handling Disputed Information in Commercial Debtor Files

While it is not required by law, Federal agencies should handle disputed information from their commercial debtors in the same manner as consumer disputes (see Chapter 2). Disputed information should be investigated and resolved in a prompt and timely manner. The credit reporting agency contacts listed on **Appendix 3** are available to assist with dispute resolution.

Commercial Account Data Elements
(*) Designates required field

Identification Elements

*(1) Account Number: Each debt must have a unique account number. This should be the discrete alphabetic, numeric or alpha-numeric code which identifies each individual debt.

Codes which are based primarily on Social Security Numbers or Employer Identification Numbers are acceptable only if the agency can distinguish between different debts which may have been made or other types of credit which may have been extended to a single entity and if otherwise authorized by law. An additional character added to the code could be used to make such distinctions. In order to avoid potential reporting errors, account numbers should not be re-used or re-issued once an account has been closed.

*(2)   Taxpayer Identification Number (TIN): This is the number used to identify individuals and businesses by the Internal Revenue Service (e.g., Social Security Numbers and Employer Identification Numbers). In accordance with the DCIA and OMB Circular No. A-129, agencies are required to obtain the TIN of all persons or entities with whom it does business. See 31 U.S.C. § 7701(c). When transmitting files to a credit reporting agency, the TIN can be omitted **only** if the agency has exhausted all means to obtain it. **NOTE**: Delinquent debts should be reported even if agencies are unable to locate and provide a TIN. In instances where the TIN is not available, this field of the reporting format submitted to the credit reporting agency should be zero filled.

*(3)   Name: This should identify the individual(s) or entity who is primarily legally liable to repay the debt. Agencies should require the debtor to notify them of any changes to legal liability. Agencies should maintain the name(s) and address(es) of the debtor(s) of record, guarantors, and any other legally liable parties.

*(4)   Address: This should be the address of the principal residence or place of business of the legally liable individual(s) or entity which corresponds to the reported name, including city, state and zip code. A street address should be provided; route numbers and/ or post office boxes should be avoided whenever possible.

Debt Elements

*(5)   Type of Debt: Report the type of debt (e.g., loan, overpayment, fee, fine, penalty, claim, forfeiture, rent, royalty, damages, audit disallowance, sale of goods or services, advances for services or goods no longer required, miscellaneous, or other).

*(6)   Date Debt Initiated: In the case of a loan or line of credit, this is the date when the Government made the legal commitment to extend credit. If this date is unavailable, report the date of the initial disbursement of funds or the date of the loan closing, whichever is earlier. For other types of debt, the date to be provided is the date the debt was created or assessed. For example, use the date of sale if the debt arose as the result of an installment sale, or date of assessment in the case of a fine or fee. The date that the debtor was notified of the debt should not be used unless this is the date the debt was established (e.g., certain administrative debt).

* (7)   Amount of Debt: Report the full amount of the original debt, principal only. (Report dollars only)

(8)   Maturity Date: Report the date by which the debt is due to be repaid in full.

(9)   Frequency: Report how often payment is made (e.g., monthly, quarterly, semi-annually, annually, or irregularly.)

(10)   Security: Report a loan as "Secured" (or "S") if collateral had to be pledged as part of the original loan agreement and the value of the collateral is known to be equal to or greater than the full loan amount. In any other circumstance, this category should be left blank.

**Current Activity
Elements (Status Codes)**

(11)   Status: Report the current status of the debt as identified below:

(a)   current -- payments are up-to-date, and the account is in good standing.

(b)   delinquent -- indicates that at least one repayment of the loan or debt is overdue. This classification should be used when there is no other status which better describes the account.

(c)   in default -- indicates 90 or more days past due.

(d)   in collection -- account has been assigned to an attorney, collection agency, an agency's internal collection department.

(e)   contested -- terms or amounts are in dispute; however, case has not gone into formal proceedings.

(f)   in litigation – court proceedings are pending.

(g)   foreclosure started -- proceedings which will lead to foreclosure have been undertaken. The term "forcclosure" is usually used for mortgaged property.

(h)   foreclosed -- foreclosure has been completed.

(i)   repossessed collateral -- collateral has been repossessed, either voluntarily or involuntarily.

(j)   written off /currently not collectible -- amount of loan or debt has been written off, however the Agency has determined to continue to pursue further collection efforts.

(k)   settled -- (compromised) account legally paid for less than full balance and the debtor has no further legal obligation.

(l)   paid in full -- account repaid in accordance with agreement, no outstanding balance due.

(m)   paid in full/was in collection -- account has now been paid, although it had gone to collection.

(n)   paid in full/written off -- account has now been paid, although the account had been previously written off.

(o)   paid in full/was repossession -- account has now been paid, although repossession had occurred.

(p)   cannot be located -- entity has gone out of business or cannot be found at any address.

(q)   written off/closed-out or discharged - collection action has terminated and no further collection efforts are warranted. Account was reported to IRS on Form 1099C.

(r)   other (specify).

Since these classifications are not intended to be mutually exclusive, more than one may apply in some situations; however, **the classification reported should be the one which most accurately reflects the current collection activity of an account.**

Some status classifications must be considered to override others. The following are such classifications, in order of priority; (a) debtor cannot be located; (b) account has been foreclosed; and, (c) in litigation. Information on bankruptcies will be obtained by credit reporting agencies from public records and included on the appropriate credit report. "In bankruptcy" is not to be reported by agencies as an account's status. "In collection" should be reported instead.

(12) Amount of Debt Outstanding: The amount to be reported is the total amount currently owed on the debt, including all interest and late fees.

(13) Past Due Amount: The amount to be reported is the amount which is overdue, including financing interest and all late charges.

(14) Date of Most Recent Payment: Report the most recent date on which payment was received. If no payment has been received, leave blank.

(15) Date of Violation: This is the date on which the most recent violation of the agreement occurred, if applicable. If the violation is a delinquency, report the date the debt became delinquent. If a grace period is given for payment (e.g., 30 days after the due date before additional charges are levied), the debt becomes delinquent if the period ends without payment. However, the date of delinquency is the original due date, not the date which designates the end of the grace period.

**Agency Identification
Elements**

  (16) <u>Contact Person</u>: Report the name and telephone number for the individual designated as contact for the lending agency or division responsible for handling the debt.

  *(17) <u>Federal Creditor Agency</u>: Report the department, or agency, and if available, the sub-agency and the program under which the lending or other credit/debt activity occurred.

Reporting Commercial Account Information

SUMMARY

1. Execute MOU with each commercial credit reporting agency accepting Federal data on commercial debtors (See Sample MOU at **Appendix 2**).

2.. Contact each of the commercial credit reporting agencies receiving Federal debtor data to establish a reporting relationship (contacts, addresses, etc.). Federal agencies are reminded that data is to be sent on a non-exclusive basis (all data is to be sent to **each** of the commercial credit reporting agencies). See **Appendix 3** for credit reporting agency contacts.

3. Agree to method and media in which data will be sent (magnetic tape, disks, electronic, etc.).

4. Prepare/format data for submission to credit reporting agencies. The Commercial Reporting Format is contained in Chapter 3.

5. Complete "Transmittal of Account Information" sheet to accompany tape, etc.

6. Submit data to credit reporting agencies. The credit reporting agencies will return all tapes to the respective agency after the data has been loaded into their database. Agencies are encouraged to work with the credit reporting agencies to develop a method to determine whether debtor data has been loaded into their database and is being properly reported.

AUTOMATED REPORTING FORMAT FOR COMMERCIAL DEBT

OLD DATA FIELD	NEW DATA FIELD	RELATED DATA ELEMENT	POSITION	FIELD SIZE	FIELD TYPE	NOTE
G	G					
Contributor Number	Contributor Number		2-7	6	N	Requested/ Assigned by Credit Reporting Agency
Filler	Filler		8-11	4	-	
*Name of Debtor - 1	*Name of debtor-1	*(3) Name	12-51	40	AN	
*Name of Debtor - 2	*Name of Debtor-2		52-91	40	AN	
*Address -1	*Address -1	*(4) Address	92-121	30	AN	
*Address -2	*Address -2		122-151	30	AN	
Filler	Filler		152-156	5	-	
"1" or "2"	"1" or "2"		157	1	N	Special Comments, #1
*City	*City		158-177	20	AN	
*State	*State		178-193	16	AN	Special Comments, #2
*Zip Code	*Zip Code		194-202	9	N	
State Abbreviation	State Abbreviation		203-204	2	A	
Filler	Filler		205-207	3	-	
Date of Report	Date of Report		208-213	6	N	Date Reported to Credit Reporting Agency
*Account Number	*Account Number	*(1) Account Number	214-233	20	AN	
*Taxpayer Identification Number	*Taxpayer Identification Number	*(2) Taxpayer Identification Number	234-242	9	N	
* Federal Agency	* Federal Agency	*(17) Federal Creditor Agency	243-254	3	A	Appendix 5
* Federal Sub-Agency	* Federal Sub-Agency		246-248	3	AN	Special Comments #3
* Program Code	* Program Code		249-252	4	N	Special Comments #4
Responsible Person	Contact Person	(16) Contact Person				
- Name	- Name		253-272	20	AN	
- Phone	- Phone		273-282	10	N	Include Area Code
Rescheduled # of Times	Dropped		283-284	2	N	"0" Fill

AUTOMATED REPORTING FORMAT FOR COMMERCIAL DEBT

OLD DATA FIELD	NEW DATA FIELD	RELATED DATA ELEMENT	POSITION	FIELD SIZE	FIELD TYPE	NOTE
Status	Status	(11) Status	285	1	A	Table 1
If status is "R", explain	If status is "R," explain		286-300	15	AN	
Frequency of Payment	Frequency	(9) Frequency	301	1	A	Table 2
Interest						
- Computation	Dropped		302-309	8	AN	"0" fill
- Percent	Dropped		310-313	4	A	"0" Fill
Most Recent Payment	Date of Most Recent Payment	(14) Date of Most Recent Payment	314-319	6	N	
Current Balance	Current Balance	(12) Amount of Debt Outstanding	320-331	12	N	
Current Amount Due	Dropped		332-343	12	N	"O" Fill
Past Due Amount	Past Due Amount	(13) Past Due Amount	344-355	12	N	
Date of Occurrence	Date of Violation	(15) Date of Violation	356-361	6	N	
Late Charges						
- Interest	Dropped		362	1	A	"0" Fill
- Administrative Costs	Dropped		363	1	A	"0" Fill
- Penalties	Dropped		364	1	A	"0" Fill
*Amount	*Amount of Debt	*(7) Amount of Debt	365-376	12	N	
*Type of Loan	*Type of Debt	*(5)Type of Debt	377-378	2	A	Table 3
Percent Guaranteed	Dropped		379-383	5	N	"0" Fill
*Award Date	*Date Debt Initiated	*(6) Date Debt Initiated	384-389	6	N	
Maturity Date	Maturity Date	(8) Maturity Date	390-395	6	N	
Security	Security	(10) Security	396	1	N	"S" if Secured
Amount Disbursed	Dropped		397-408	12	N	"0"Filled
Private Lender	Dropped		409-443	35	AN	"0" Fill
Multi-Liable Parties	Dropped		444-445	2	N	"0" Fill
Filler	Filler		446-500	55	-	

Comments and Tables

Technical Comments

1. Header and trailer records, as requested by the credit reporting agency, may be supplied.

2. The fields for those categories requiring dates should be completely filled. For example, January 1, 2001, would be entered as 010101.

3. Alpha fields should be right or left justified and zero (0) filled; numeric fields should be right justified and zero (0) filled.

4. If data is not available for a specific numeric item of information, then fill the field with nine(s) (9s). If data is not available for a specific alpha item of information, blank fill the field.

5. Round cents to the nearest dollar. For example, a debt of $110.50 would be reported as 000000000111.

6. Unless otherwise noted, omit all special characters.

Special Comments

1. The number one (1) in this field indicates that the city/state information which follows is contained in separate fields. The number two (2) in this field indicates that the city/state information which follows is contained in the same field.

2. Either the full name of the state or its abbreviation may be provided.

3. This three (3) digit code will be determined by the agency and provided to the credit reporting agencies.

4. The four (4) digit numeric code to be used in this field is the appropriation code, which is the same as the account code used by the Department of the Treasury for the Monthly Treasury Statement.

Table 1

CURRENT ACTIVITY STATUS CODES

CODE	EXPLANATION
A	Current
B	Delinquent
C	In Default
D	In Collection
E	Contested
F	In Litigation
G	Foreclosure Started
H	Foreclosed
I	Repossessed Collateral
J	Written Off/Currently Not Collectible
K	Settled
L	Paid In Full
M	Paid In Full/Was Collection
N	Paid In Full/Written Off
O	Paid In Full/Was Repossession
P	Cannot be Located
Q	Written Off/Closed-Out or Discharged
R	Other (Specify)

*If "R", use positions 286-300 to explain

Table 2

FREQUENCY OF PAYMENT

CODE	EXPLANATION
M	Monthly
Q	Quarterly
S	Semi-Annually
A	Annually
I	Irregularly

Table 3

TYPE OF DEBT

CODE	EXPLANATION		CODE	EXPLANATION
LN	Loan		RE	Rent
OV	Overpayment		RO	Royalty
FE	Fee		DM	Damages
FI	Fine		AD	Audit Disallowances
PN	Penalty		SA	Sales
CL	Claim		AV	Advances
FO	Forfeiture		MI	Miscellaneous
OT	Other			

SECTION 3711(e) OF TITLE 31, UNITED STATES CODE

Title 31, MONEY AND FINANCE
SUBTITLE III - FINANCIAL MANAGEMENT
CHAPTER 37 -- CLAIMS

SUBCHAPTER 11-- CLAIMS OF THE UNITED STATES GOVERNMENT

31 U.S.C. § 3711

31 U.S.C. § 3711. Collection and Compromise

***

(e)(1) When trying to collect a claim of the Government under a law except the Internal Revenue Code of 1986 (26 U.S.C. § 1 et seq.), the head of an executive, judicial, or legislative agency shall disclose to a consumer reporting agency information from a system of records that a person is responsible for a claim if–

(A) notice required by section 552a(e)(4) of title 5 indicates that information in the system maybe disclosed to a consumer reporting agency;

(B) the head of the agency has reviewed the claim and decided that the claim is valid and overdue;

(C) the head of the agency has notified the person in writing--

  (i) that payment of the claim is overdue;

  (ii) that, within not less than 60 days after sending the notice, the head of the agency intends to disclose to a consumer reporting agency that the person is responsible for the claim;

  (iii) of the specific information to be disclosed to the consumer reporting agency; and

  (iv) of the rights the person has to a complete explanation of the claim, to dispute information in the records of the agency about the claim, and to administrative repeal or review of the claim;

(D) the person has not--

31 U.S.C. § 3711 (cont.)

   (i) repaid or agreed to repay the claim under a written repayment plan that the person has signed and the head of the agency has agreed to; or

   (ii) filed for review of the claim under paragraph (2) of this subsection;

(E) the head of the agency has established procedures to–

   (i) disclose promptly, to reach consumer reporting agency to which the original disclosure was made, a substantial change in the condition or amount of the claim;

   (ii) verify or correct promptly information about the claim on request of a consumer reporting agency for verification of information disclosed; and

   (iii) get satisfactory assurances from each consumer reporting agency that the agency is complying with all laws of the United States related to providing consumer credit information; and

(F) the information disclosed to the consumer reporting agency is limited to--

   (i) information necessary to establish the identity of the person, including name, address, and taxpayer identification number;

   (ii) the amount, status, and history of the claim; and

   (iii) the agency or program under which the claim arose.

(2) Before disclosing information to a consumer reporting agency under paragraph (1) of this subsection and at other times allowed by law, the head of an executive, judicial, or legislative agency shall provide, on request of a person alleged by the agency to be responsible for the claim, for a review of the obligation of the person, including an opportunity for reconsideration of the initial decision on the claim.

(3) Before disclosing information to a consumer reporting agency under paragraph (1) of this subsection, the head of an executive, judicial, or legislative agency shall take reasonable action to locate a person for whom the head of the agency does not have a current address to send the notice under paragraph (1)(c).

31 U.S.C. § 3711 (cont.)

(4) The head of each executive agency shall require, as a condition for insuring or guaranteeing any loan, financing, or other extension of credit under any law to a person, that the lender provide information relating to the extension of credit to consumer reporting agencies or commercial reporting agencies, as appropriate.

(5) The head of each executive agency may provide to a consumer reporting agency or commercial reporting agency information from a system of records that a person is responsible for a claim which is current, if notice required by section 552a(e)(4) of title 5 indicates that information in the system may be disclosed to a consumer reporting agency or commercial reporting agency, respectively.

***

Page left intentionally blank

(MODEL)

MEMORANDA OF UNDERSTANDING

FOR

REPORTING OF CONSUMER AND COMMERCIAL DEBTS

MEMORANDUM OF UNDERSTANDING
For the Reporting of Consumer Debt

Introduction

This Memorandum of Understanding (MOU) is entered into by and between the undersigned credit reporting agency (hereinafter referred to as Credit Agency) and Federal agency (hereinafter referred to as the Government). This MOU is entered into in order to carry out the purposes of the Debt Collection Act of 1982 (DCA), as amended by the Debt Collection Improvement Act of 1996 (DCIA) and codified at 31 U.S.C. § 3711(e), which governs Federal agency reporting of debt information to credit reporting agencies. This MOU is consistent with the implementing guidelines of the DCA and DCIA, including the Federal Claims Collection Standards (31 C.F.R. § 901.4), OMB Circular A-129, and the Treasury Guide to the Federal Credit Bureau Program.

Operating Terms and Conditions

The Credit Agency and the Government hereto agree as follows:

A. **Except as provided in Sections B and D below, the Government will:**

1. Report, on a non-exclusive basis, information on its consumer debts (Account Information) as described in the "Guide to the Federal Credit Bureau Program" (Guide).

2. Verify the accuracy of the Account Information in accordance with the DCA and DCIA and its standard procedures for debt verification before reporting the Account Information to the Credit Agency.

3. Provide Account Information on a monthly basis to the individual or position designated in writing by the Credit Agency once notified by the Credit Agency that the initial submission has been loaded. The Government will prepare the information in the Associated Credit Bureaus Inc. METRO 2 format. (See Chapter 2 of the Guide - "Reporting Consumer Account Information" for instructions on downloading the Metro 2 format).

4. Prepare the Account Information in the format mutually agreed to by both parties, on magnetic tape, manually, or in any other form agreed to by both parties, and bear the cost of preparing and providing the Account Information to the Credit Agency.

A-6

5. Send, under separate cover, a completed transmittal letter (form attached as <u>Attachment A</u>) to the Credit Agency to inform it of the type, number and amount of accounts included in the Account Information being submitted, prior to, or concurrent with, the transmittal of the Account Information.

6. Use reasonable efforts to provide prompt, accurate and complete Account Information to the Credit Agency.

7. Investigate disputes and correct any erroneous Account Information promptly, in accordance with the DCA and the DCIA.

8. Allow the Credit Agency to supply the Account Information to other credit agencies consistent with applicable laws, so long as the Credit Agency supplies any such credit agencies with the appropriate Government contact names, addresses and phone numbers as the Government designates in writing and as may change from time to time.

B.   The Government will not:

1. Be obligated to provide Account Information to the Credit Agency if it finds that the Credit Agency is not loading the information into a data file and making it available on credit reports that the Credit Agency produces.

2. Be liable to or indemnify the Credit Agency for any damages whatsoever arising from the Government's failure to provide any Account Information, or if it fails to provide the Account Information at any stated times.

C.   Except as Provided in Section D Below, The Credit Agency Will:

1. Within thirty (30) calendar days of receipt of the first submission of Account Information, and within ten (10) business days of each subsequent submission, incorporate the Account Information into its data files, credit reports, and other business information products and services so long as the Credit Agency has no reason to believe that the Account Information is inaccurate.

2. Provide the Government with exception reports listing which accounts have not been or could not be loaded into the data files and the reason(s) therefore within seven (7) business days of receipt of the Account Information.

3. Return, at its own cost, any magnetic tapes, computer disks, or other physical media, which the Government used to transmit Account Information, within ten (10) business days of loading the Account Information contained in such media.

4. Notify the Government that it has received the Account Information within three (3) business days of such receipt by returning the "Receipt Acknowledgment" portion of the transmittal letter sent with the transmittal to the individual or office indicated therein or in such other manner as agreed to by the parties.

5. Comply at all times with all laws and regulations applicable to its operation as a credit reporting agency.

6. Within thirty (30) days of being notified that any Account Information is erroneous, the Credit Reporting Agency will correct or delete the Account Information and, pursuant to section 611(7)(d) of the Fair Credit Reporting Act, will send notice of any such correction or deletion of information to any previous consumer report recipients identified and requested by the consumer, which may include credit grantors and other consumer reporting agencies, as well as to any other credit reporting agency to which the Credit Reporting Agency supplied such erroneous information.

7. Supply any and all credit reporting agencies receiving any Account Information from the Credit Reporting Agency with the contact names and phone numbers contained in the "Notices" section herein for purposes of notifying the Government about any disputes about the Account Information.

8. Furnish an executed copy of this MOU to the Department of the Treasury, Financial Management Service (FMS), Debt Management Services, Manager, Credit Bureau Reporting Program at 401 14th Street, SW - Room 446, Washington, DC 20227.

General

D.   The parties expressly acknowledge and agree that:

1. Any Account Information furnished by the Government shall be used solely to integrate that information with similar information received from other private and public sector sources. This information will be distributed by the Credit Reporting Agency consistent with appropriate Federal laws. It shall not be used, sold, given, loaned or otherwise furnished to any entity except the customers of the Credit Reporting Agency, the consumer who is the subject of the information, or other credit bureaus.

2. The Government will not be liable to the Credit Reporting Agency for any damages as a result of any failure to respond to the Credit Reporting Agency's request to validate previously reported Account Information within the required time period.

3. In the event that a third party brings a claim against the Credit Reporting Agency, the Credit Reporting Agency will not bring a claim, in any form or at any time, against the Government, its employees, or officers for the cost or liabilities incurred by the Credit

Reporting Agency defending any such claim.

4. In the event that a third party brings a claim against the Government, the Government shall not bring a claim against a Credit Reporting Agency, its employees or officers for the costs or liabilities incurred by the Government, except as provided in Paragraphs 5 and 10 below. The claims barred by this paragraph and paragraph B.2., above, include, without limitations, any claims for breach of contract, tortious injury, violation of constitutional entitlement, contribution, statutory law or common law, contractual or equitable indemnity.

5. The Credit Reporting Agency will indemnify the Government for any loss or damage, including attorney's fees and costs, sustained by the Government as a result of the Credit Reporting Agency's negligent, reckless or wilful use of any Account Information in a way or for a purpose not authorized or contemplated by this MOU.

6. The Government's failure to respond to requests for verification of any Account Information disputed by the debtor within the time period established by law, regulation or this MOU may result in the complete elimination of the disputed account from the Credit Reporting Agency's files.

7. The Government does not warrant the accuracy or completeness of the Account Information reported to the Credit Reporting Agency and shall not be liable or responsible for any loss or damage incurred by this Credit Reporting Agency or any other credit reporting agency or bureau to which this Credit Reporting Agency supplies information for any incomplete or inaccurate data.

8. There will be no payment by either party to the other for any services performed by the Credit Reporting Agency as specified herein.

9. The duties, rights and obligations of the parties pursuant to this MOU are solely limited to the terms of this MOU. The Credit Reporting Agency is not, in any circumstances, the agent, employee, servant, or deputy of the Government; nor shall the Credit Reporting Agency make representations, actual or implied, thereof.

10. The Credit Reporting Agency will indemnify the Government for any damages whatsoever arising out of an administrative or judicial finding that the Credit Reporting Agency is the actual or apparent agency, employee, servant or deputy of the Government.

11. The Government and the Credit Reporting Agency each agree to furnish to FMS a "Quarterly Report on Credit Reporting Agency Activity" (in the form found in Attachment B) on April 15, July 15, October 15, and January 15 of each year. If any of these dates is not a business day, the report will be furnished on the next business day. As indicated on Attachment B, the report shall describe the number of accounts referred by the Government, the dollar value of the accounts (if known), and the number of

accounts returned as unprocessible to the Government. The report shall only cover accounts reported by the Government and received by the Credit Reporting Agency during the last month of the Government's quarterly reporting cycle. (I.e., data should be reported for the months of March, June, September and December.) The Credit Reporting Agency may combine this report with the quarterly reports for other Federal agencies' consumer debt accounts.

Termination

Either party may terminate this MOU by providing thirty (30) calendar days written notice to the other party as set forth under "Notices" below. In the event that the Government terminates this MOU, it will request the return of any tapes then at the Credit Reporting Agency. The Credit Reporting Agency agrees to delete all information supplied by the Government from its data files within thirty (30) days of the date of termination if the Government requests that such information be deleted.

Notices

All notices required to be made pursuant to this MOU shall be made in writing to the contacts named below.

A.   Inquiries or notifications regarding the Account Information shall be directed to:

Name:
Title:
Office:
Address:
Phone:
Fax.:
E-mail:

B.   Notice of Termination of this MOU or any other communications regarding the performance of this MOU shall be directed to:

Name:
Title:
Office:
Address:
Phone:
Fax.:
E-mail:

Effective Date

This MOU supercedes all previous agreements and shall commence on the date of signature by the Government or on the effective date of the General Services Administration's Federal Supply Schedule for obtaining credit reports, whichever is later. Unless sooner terminated by either party, this MOU shall terminate on the effective termination date of said Federal Supply Schedule.

In witness whereof, the Credit Reporting Agency and the Government have caused this MOU to be executed in multiple counterparts by their duly authorized representatives as indicated below. Each signatory represents and warrants, under penalty of perjury, to the best of his/her knowledge and belief, that it has the delegated authority to sign on behalf of and legally obligate the agency that each represents. If more than one Federal agency signs this agreement, the signature of one Government agency will not bind any other signatory agency.

GOVERNMENT:

By: _____ Date:_____

Name: _____
             (print name)

Title: _____

Federal Agency:_____

Credit Reporting Agency:

By: _____ Date:_____

Name: _____
             (print name)
Title: _____

Company:_____

SAMPLE

TRANSMITTAL OF ACCOUNT INFORMATION
DATE TRANSMITTED:_____

TO: (full name and address)   FROM: (full name and address)

Agency/bureau transmitting data: _____

Type of accounts (circle one)   consumer   commercial

Number of accounts:_____

Dollar Value of Accounts:_____

Questions? Contact:_____
                              (name, phone number)

        E-mail: _____ Fax: _____

RECEIPT ACKNOWLEDGMENT

Agency: _____

Received by Credit Reporting Agency on: _____
                                                          (date)

By: (signature)   _____

        (printed)   _____

Questions? Contact:_____
                              (name, phone number)

        E-mail:_____ Fax:_____

                                        Agency return address
                                        here to show through
                                        window envelope

A-12

Quarterly Report on Credit Reporting Agency Activity

Type of Accounts: ( ) Commercial   ( ) Consumer

Reporting Period _____, 20____

AGENCY REPORTING	# OF ACCOUNTS REFERRED/PROCESSED	DOLLAR VALUE OF ACCOUNTS (IF AVAILABLE)	# OF ACCOUNTS RETURNED/ UNPROCESSED

SUBMIT TO: Department of the Treasury
                     Financial Management Service
                     Debt Management Services
                     401 14th Street, SW - Rm. 446
                     ATTN: Credit Bureau Reporting Project
                     Washington, D.C. 20227

SUBMITTED BY: _____
                            NAME

                     _____
                           AGENCY

                     _____
                          TELEPHONE

                     _____
                           E-MAIL

**(MODEL)
MEMORANDUM OF UNDERSTANDING
For the Reporting of Commercial Debt**

Introduction

This Memorandum of Understanding (MOU) is entered into by and between the undersigned credit reporting agency (hereinafter referred to as Credit Reporting Agency) and Federal agency (hereinafter referred to as the Government). This MOU is entered into in order to carry out the purposes of the Debt Collection Act of 1982 (DCA), as amended by the Debt Collection Improvement Act of 1996 (DCIA) and codified at 31 U.S.C. § 3711(e), which govern Federal agency reporting of debt information to credit reporting agencies. This MOU is consistent with the implementing guidelines of the DCA and DCIA, including the Federal Claims Collection Standards (31 C.F.R. § 901.4), OMB Circular A-129, and the Treasury "Guide to the Federal Credit Bureau Program."

Operating Terms and Conditions

The Credit Reporting Agency and the Government hereto agree as follows:

A.   Except as provided in Sections B and D below, the Government will:

1.   Report, on a non-exclusive basis, information on its commercial debts (Account Information) as described in the "Guide to the Federal Credit Bureau Program" (Guide).

2.   Verify the accuracy of the Account Information in accordance with the DCA and DCIA and its standard procedures for debt verification before reporting the Account Information to the Credit Reporting Agency.

3.   Provide Account Information on a quarterly basis to the individual or position designated in writing by the Credit Reporting Agency.

4.   Prepare the Account Information in the format mutually agreed to by both parties, on magnetic tape, manually, or in any other form agreed to by both parties, and bear the cost of preparing and providing the Account Information to the Credit Reporting Agency. (See Chapter 3 of the Guide for Commercial reporting format.)

5. Send, under separate cover, a completed transmittal letter (form attached as <u>Attachment A</u>) to the Credit Reporting Agency to inform it of the type, number and amount of accounts included in the Account Information being submitted, prior to, or concurrent with, the transmittal of the Account Information.

6. Use reasonable efforts to provide prompt, accurate and complete Account Information to the Credit Reporting Agency.

7. Investigate disputes and correct any erroneous Account Information promptly, in accordance with the DCA and the DCIA.

8. Allow the Credit Reporting Agency to supply the Account Information to other credit agencies consistent with applicable laws, so long as the Credit Reporting Agency supplies any such credit agencies with the appropriate Government contact names, addresses and phone numbers as the Government designates in writing and as may change from time to time.

B. The Government will not:

1. Be obligated to provide Account Information to the Credit Reporting Agency if it finds that the Credit Reporting Agency is not loading the information into a data file and making it available on credit reports that the Credit Reporting Agency produces.

2. Be liable to or indemnify the Credit Reporting Agency for any damages whatsoever arising from the Government's failure to provide any Account Information, or if it fails to provide the Account Information at any stated times.

C. Except as Provided in Section D Below, The Credit Reporting Agency Will:

1. Within thirty (30) calendar days of receipt of the first submission of Account Information, and within ten (10) business days of each subsequent submission, incorporate the Account Information into its data files, credit reports, and other business information products and services so long as the Credit Reporting Agency has no reason to believe that the Account Information is inaccurate.

2. Provide the Government with exception reports listing which accounts have not been or could not be loaded into the data files and the reason(s) therefore within seven (7) business days of receipt of the Account Information.

3. Return, at its own cost, any magnetic tapes, computer disks, or other physical media, which the Government used to transmit Account Information, within ten (10) business days of loading the Account Information contained in such media.

4. Notify the Government that it has received the Account Information within three (3) business days of such receipt by returning the "Receipt Acknowledgment" portion of the transmittal letter sent with the transmittal to the individual or office indicated therein, or in such other manner as agreed to by the parties.

5. Comply at all times with all laws and regulations applicable to its operation as a credit reporting agency.

6. Within thirty (30) days of being notified that any Account Information is erroneous, notify any credit reporting agency to which the Credit Reporting Agency supplied such erroneous information that the Account Information was erroneous and must be corrected.

7. Supply any and all credit reporting agencies receiving any Account Information from the Credit Reporting Agency with the contact names and phone numbers contained in the "Notices" section herein for purposes of notifying the Government about any disputes about the Account Information.

8. Furnish an executed copy of this MOU to the Department of the Treasury, Financial Management Service, Debt Management Services, Manager, Credit Bureau Reporting Program at 401 14th Street, SW - Room 446, Washington, DC 20227.

General

D. **The parties expressly acknowledge and agree that:**

1. Any Account Information furnished by the Government shall be used solely to integrate that information with similar information received from other private and public sector sources. This information will be distributed by the Credit Reporting Agency consistent with appropriate Federal laws. It shall not be used, sold, given, loaned or otherwise furnished to any entity except the customers of the Credit Reporting Agency, the consumer who is the subject of the information, or other credit bureaus.

2. The Government will not be liable to the Credit Reporting Agency for any damages as a result of any failure to respond to the Credit Reporting Agency's request to validate previously reported Account Information within the required time period.

3. In the event that a third party brings a claim against the Credit Reporting Agency, the Credit Reporting Agency will not bring a claim, in any form or at any time, against the Government, its employees, or officers for the cost or liabilities incurred by the Credit Reporting Agency defending any such claim.

4.	In the event that a third party brings a claim against the Government, the Government shall not bring a claim against a Credit Reporting Agency, its employees or officers for the costs or liabilities incurred by the Government, except as provided in Paragraphs 5 and 10 below. The claims barred by this paragraph and paragraph B.2., above, include, without limitations, any claims for breach of contract, tortuous injury, violation of constitutional entitlement, contribution, statutory law or common law, contractual or equitable indemnity.

5.	The Credit Reporting Agency will indemnify the Government for any loss or damage, including attorney's fees and costs, sustained by the Government as a result of the Credit Reporting Agency's negligent, reckless or wilful use of any Account Information in a way or for a purpose not authorized or contemplated by this MOU.

6.	The Government's failure to respond to requests for verification of any Account Information disputed by the debtor within the time period established by law, regulation or this MOU may result in the complete elimination of the disputed account from the Credit Reporting Agency's files.

7.	The Government does not warrant the accuracy or completeness of the Account Information reported to the Credit Reporting Agency and shall not be liable or responsible for any loss or damage incurred by this Credit Reporting Agency or any other credit reporting agency or bureau to which this Credit Reporting Agency supplies information for any incomplete or inaccurate data.

8.	There will be no payment by either party to the other for any services performed by the Credit Reporting Agency as specified herein.

9.	The duties, rights and obligations of the parties pursuant to this MOU are solely limited to the terms of this MOU. The Credit Reporting Agency is not, in any circumstances, the agent, employee, servant, or deputy of the Government; nor shall the Credit Reporting Agency make representations, actual or implied, thereof.

10.	The Credit Reporting Agency will indemnify the Government for any damages whatsoever arising out of an administrative or judicial finding that the Credit Reporting Agency is the actual or apparent agency, employee, servant or deputy of the Government.

11.	The Government and the Credit Reporting Agency each agree to furnish to FMS a "Quarterly Report on Credit Reporting Agency Activity" (in the form found in Attachment B) on April 15, July 15, October 15, and January 15 of each year. If any of these dates is not a business day, the report will be furnished on the next business day. As indicated on Attachment B, the report shall describe the number of accounts referred by the Government, the dollar value of the accounts (if known), and the number of accounts returned as unprocessible to the Government. The report shall only cover accounts reported by the Government and received by the Credit Reporting Agency during the last month of the Government's quarterly reporting cycle. (I.e., data should be reported for the months of March, June, September and December.) The Credit Reporting Agency may combine this report with the quarterly reports for other Federal agencies' commercial debt accounts.

Termination

Either party may terminate this MOU by providing thirty (30) calendar days written notice to the other party as set forth under "Notices" below. In the event that the Government terminates this MOU, it will request the return of any tapes then at the Credit Reporting Agency. The Credit Reporting Agency agrees to delete all information supplied by the Government from its data files within thirty (30) days of the date of termination if the Government requests that such information be deleted.

Notices

All notices required to be made pursuant to this MOU shall be made in writing to the contacts named below.

A.   Inquiries or notifications regarding the Account Information shall be directed to:

Name:
Title:
Office:
Address:
Phone:
Fax.:
E-mail:

B.   Notice of Termination of this MOU or any other communications regarding the performance of this MOU shall be directed to:

Name:
Title:
Office:
Address:
Phone:
Fax.:
E-mail:

Effective Date

This MOU supercedes all previous agreements and shall commence on the date of signature by the Government or on the effective date of the General Services Administration's Federal Supply Schedule for obtaining credit reports, whichever is later. Unless sooner terminated by either party, this MOU shall terminate on the effective termination date of said Federal Supply Schedule.

In witness whereof, the Credit Reporting Agency and the Government have caused this MOU to be executed in multiple counterparts by their duly authorized representatives as indicated below. Each signatory represents and warrants, under penalty of perjury, to the best of his/her knowledge and belief, that it has the delegated authority to sign on behalf of and legally obligate the agency that each represents. If more than one Federal agency signs this agreement, the signature of one Government agency will not bind any other signatory agency.

GOVERNMENT:

By: _____   Date:_____

Name: _____
               (print name)
Title: _____

Federal Agency:_____

Credit Reporting Agency:

By: _____   Date:_____

Name: _____
               (print name)
Title: _____

Company: _____

<u>SAMPLE</u>

TRANSMITTAL OF ACCOUNT INFORMATION
DATE TRANSMITTED:_____

TO: (full name and address)   FROM: (full name and address)

Agency/bureau transmitting data: _____

Type of accounts (circle one)   consumer   commercial

Number of accounts:_____

Dollar Value of Accounts:_____

Questions? Contact:_____
                      (name, phone number)

          E-mail: _____Fax: _____

RECEIPT ACKNOWLEDGMENT

Agency: _____

Received by Repository/Credit Bureau on: _____
                                              (date)

By: (signature)   _____
     (printed)   _____

Questions? Contact:_____
                      (name, phone number)

          E-mail: _____ Fax:_____

                              Agency return address
                              here to show through window envelope

Quarterly
Report on Credit Reporting Agency Activity

Type of Accounts: ( ) Commercial   ( ) Consumer

REPORTING AGENCY	# OF ACCOUNTS REFERRED	DOLLAR VALUE OF ACCOUNTS (If Available)	# OF ACCOUNTS RETURNED/UNPROCESSED

SUBMIT TO: Department of the Treasury
                           Financial Management Service
                           Debt Management Services
                           401 14th Street, SW - Rm. 446
                           ATTN: Credit Bureau Reporting Project
                           Washington, D.C. 20227

SUBMITTED BY: _____
                                  NAME

                            _____
                                  AGENCY

                            _____
                                  TELEPHONE

                            _____
                                  E-MAIL

Page left intentionally blank

CREDIT REPORTING AGENCY CONTACTS (November 2005)	
DESIGNATED CREDIT REPORTING AGENCIES	
COMMERCIAL ACCOUNTS	*CONSUMER ACCOUNTS*
Dun & Bradstreet **Jeb Magruder** (610) 882-6333 (610) 807-1045 (fax) Magruderj@dnb.com **Michael Caskin** (703) 807-5076 (866) 319-9522 (fax) caskinm@dnb.com	**Experian** **Brian Lause** (714) 830-5325 (714) 830-2599 (fax) Brian.Lause@experian.com
	Equifax *Melissa Thomas** (410) 342-6765 (410) 342-6472 (fax) melissa.thomas@equifax.com
Experian **Roxie Lepich** (714) 830-5503 (714) 830-2906 (fax) Roxie.lepich@experian.com	**Trans Union** *Chad Cory** (312) 985-3024 (312) 466-7994 (fax) ccory@transunion.com
Equifax **Jeannine Suda** (770) 740-6730 (770) 740-6802 (fax) Jeannine.Suda@equifax.com	**INNOVIS Data Solutions** *Jeff Van Schoyck** (614) 326-5691 (614) 538-6102 (fax) jeff.vanschoyck@innovis.com

DEPARTMENT OF THE TREASURY - FINANCIAL MANAGEMENT SERVICE	
DEBT MANAGEMENT SERVICES-	
**DMS - Senior Analyst -Tom Kobielus	(202) 874-7359
**DMS - Senior Analyst - Matt Lorelli	(202) 874-8626
FAX Number	(202) 874-7494
DEBT MANAGEMENT SERVICES **(Debt Collection/Cross Servicing)** ***Contact: **Suzanne Renda**, Financial Program Specialist (suzanne.renda@fms.treas.gov)	(205) 912-6331 (205) 912-6322 (fax)

* New Contact
**Liaison for Federal and Credit Reporting Agencies
***Liaison for DMS-Cross-servicing of Agency Debts Transferred to Treasury for Collection

This page is left intentionally blank.

(SAMPLE)
FMS DEBT MANAGEMENT SERVICES
CROSS-SERVICING IMPLEMENTATION
AGENCY PROFILE FORM

Agency Information

Name: _____
Address Line 1:_____
Address Line 2:_____
City, State: _____
Zip Code (5 digit + 4, if known):_____

Bureau Information

Name: _____
Address Line 1: _____
Address Line 2: _____
City, State: _____
Zip Code (5 digit + 4, if known):_____
TIN _____

Bureau Office Information

Name: _____
Address Line 1: _____
Address Line 2: _____
City, State: _____
Zip Code (5 digit + 4, if known):_____
Agency Liaison Code (ALC) #: _____

	Contact Information	*Alternate Contact Information*
Name:	_____	_____
Phone No.:	_____	_____
FAX No.:	_____	_____
Email Address:	_____	_____

OPAC Contact Name

Name: _____
Phone: _____
FAX No.: _____
Email Address: _____

For FMS Use Only: Office Code _____

Program Information

Program Name (s): _____
Authorizing Statute: _____
Program Classification (Circle One)

Fines/Penalties	Business	Education	Foreign
Medical	Housing	State/Local	Other (specify name) _____

Maximum Compromise Amount: _____ *Maximum Compromise Percent: _____ *
Provide the maximum amount agency will allow Treasury to forgive without concurrence.
Statutory Authority for Compromises Greater than $100,000.00*   Yes_____   No _____
Can agency approve compromises greater than $100,000.00 without DOJ approval?
Minimum Monthly Repayment Amount (Installments): _____
Maximum Number of Months for Repayment: _____

Eligible for the Following Collection Actions (• •next to whichever applies)

Referral to Private Collection Agency (PCA)	Yes_____	No _____
Referral to Treasury Offset Program (TOP)	Yes _____	No _____
Referral to Tax Refund Offset Program (TROP), &		
Salary Offset included in Referral to TOP		
Administrative Wage Garnishment*	Yes _____	No _____

If yes, provide date and citation of hearing procedure regulation that your agency published.
_____

Credit Bureau Reporting*	Yes _____	No _____

 *If checked yes, provide name your agency used for Credit Bureau reporting.
Agency Name:_____(30 Characters)
Filing of 1099-C:
       Compromised and Discharged debts

over $600	Yes _____	No _____

   • *FMS will obtain Agency concurrence on all DOJ referrals, if checked yes.*

Additional Fees (• •next to whichever applies)

Add FMS/DMS fees to debt	Yes _____	No _____
Add Private Collection Agency (PCA) fees	Yes _____	No _____

Accruals (• •next to whichever applies)

Continue to accrue financing interest*	Yes _____	No _____
Continue to accrue late interest*	Yes _____	No _____
Continue to accrue penalty	Yes _____	No _____

An agency cannot charge both financing interest and late interest. Financing interest is interest assessed for loans.

ALL FIELDS ON THIS FORM ARE MANDATORY.
Please note: An Agency may duplicate this form as necessary to cover different requirements for different programs.

For FMS Use Only: Program Code: _____

AGENCY IDENTIFIERS
COMMONLY USED FEDERAL AGENCY CODES*

AGENCY	CODE
1. AGRICULTURE	US AGRICULTURE
2. COMMERCE	US COMMERCE
3. DEFENSE	US DEPT OF DEFENSE
4. EDUCATION	US EDUCATION
5. ENERGY	US DEPT OF ENERGY
6. HEALTH & HUMAN SERVICES	USHHS
7. HOUSING AND URBAN DEV.	USHUD
8. INTERIOR	US INTERIOR
9. JUSTICE	US JUSTICE DEPT
10. LABOR	US LABOR DEPT
11. STATE	US STATE DEPT
12. AIR FORCE	US AIR FORCE
13. ARMY	USARMY
14. NAVY	USNAVY
15. TRANSPORTATION	USDOT
16. TREASURY	USTREAS
17. VETERANS AFFAIRS	US VETERANS AFFAIRS
18. AGENCY FOR INTERNATIONAL DEV.	USAID
19. CENTRAL INTELLIGENCE AGENCY	USCIA
20. CONGRESSIONAL BUDGET OFFICE	USCBO
21. COMMODITY CREDIT CORPORATION	USCCC
22. COMMODITY FUTURES TRADING CORP	USCFTC

23. ENVIRONMENTAL PROTECTION AGENCY	USEPA
24. EXECUTIVE OFFICE OF THE PRESIDENT	USEOP
25. EXPORT-IMPORT BANK OF THE U.S.	USEXIM
26. FARM CREDIT ADMINISTRATION	USFCA
27. FEDERAL COMMUNICATIONS COMM.	USFCC
28. FEDERAL DEPOSIT INSURANCE CORP.	USFDIC
29. FEDERAL EMERGENCY MANAGEMENT AGENCY	USFEMA
30. FEDERAL TRADE COMMISSION	USFTC
31. GENERAL ACCOUNTING OFFICE	USGAO
32. GENERAL SERVICES ADMINISTRATION	USGSA
33. GOVERNMENT PRINTING OFFICE	USGPO
34. LIBRARY OF CONGRESS	USLOC
35. NAT. AERONAUTICS AND SPACE ADMIN	USNASA
36. NATIONAL ARCHIVES AND RECORDS	US NARA
37. NATIONAL CREDIT UNION ADMIN	USNCUA
38. NATIONAL SCIENCE FOUNDATION	USNSF
39. NATIONAL TRANSPORTATION SAFETY	USNTSB
40. NUCLEAR REGULATORY COMM.	USNRC
41. OFFICE OF MANAGEMENT AND BUDGET	USOMB
42. OFFICE OF PERSONNEL MANAGEMENT	USOPM
43. OTHER BOARDS AND COMMISSIONS	OTHR BOARDS CMMSNS
44. OTHER LEGISLATIVE AND JUDICIAL	OTHR LGSLTVE JUDCL
45. PENSION BENEFIT GUARANTY CORP	USPBGC
46. RAILROAD RETIREMENT BOARD	USRRB
47. SECURITIES AND EXCHANGE COMM.	USSEC
48. SMALL BUSINESS ADMINISTRATION	USSBA
49. SMITHSONIAN INSTITUTION	US SMITHSONIAN

50. SOCIAL SECURITY ADMINISTRATION	USSSA
51. TENNESSEE VALLEY AUTHORITY	USTVA
52. U.S. INFORMATION AGENCY	USINFO AGENCY
53. U.S. POSTAL SERVICE	USPOSTAL SERVICE
54. ARMY AND AIR FORCE EXCHANGE SERVICE	USAAFEXS
55. BOARD OF GOV. OF THE FED RESERVE SYSTEM	FRBGOV
56. FANNIE MAE	FANNIE MAE
57. FARM CREDIT SYSTEM	USFCS
58. FEDERAL HOME LOAN BANKS	USFHLB
59. FEDERAL RESERVE BANKS	USFRB
60. FEDERAL RETIREMENT THRIFT INVESTMENT BOARD	USFRTIB
61. FINANCING CORPORATION	US FINANCING CORP
62. FREDDIE MAC	FREDDIE MAC
63. MARINE CORPS EXCHANGE	USMCEX
64. NAVY EXCHANGE SERVICE COMMAND	USNVY SERV. COM
65. RESOLUTION FUNDING CORPORATION	USRFC
66. SALLIE MAE	SALLIE MAE
67. THRIFT SAVINGS FUND	USTSF
68. EQUAL EMPLOYMENT OPPORTUNITY	USEEOC
69. FEDERAL LABOR RELATIONS AUTHORITY	USFLRA
70. NATIONAL FOUNDATION. OF ARTS & HMNTS	USNFAH
71. CONSUMER PRODUCT SAFETY COMM.	USCPSC
72. OVERSEAS PRIVATE INVESTMENT CORP.	USOPIC
73. MARTIN LUTHER KING HOLIDAY COMM.	MLKHOLIDAY COMM
74. NEIGHBORHOOD REINVESTMENT CORP.	NREINVESTMNT CORP
75. OCCUPATIONAL SAFETY AND HEALTH REVIEW COMM.	USOSHRC
76. PANAMA CANAL COMMISSION	USPCC

77. OTHER AGENCIES	OTHER AGENCIES
78. FEDERAL ELECTION COMMISSION	USFEC
79. OFFICE OF GOVERNMENT ETHICS	USOGE
80. U.S. COURT OF VETERANS APPEALS	US COURTS VA APPEALS
81. U.S. COURTS	USCOURTS
82. TREASURY CROSS-SERVICING DEBT COLLECTION	USTREAS DMSC

*This list is not all inclusive